MINECRAFT COMIC BOOK COLLECTION

A SERIES OF AWESOME MINECRAFT COMICS

CreeperSlayer12 Series

MINECRAFT COMICS

PART 1
Journey to Minecraft

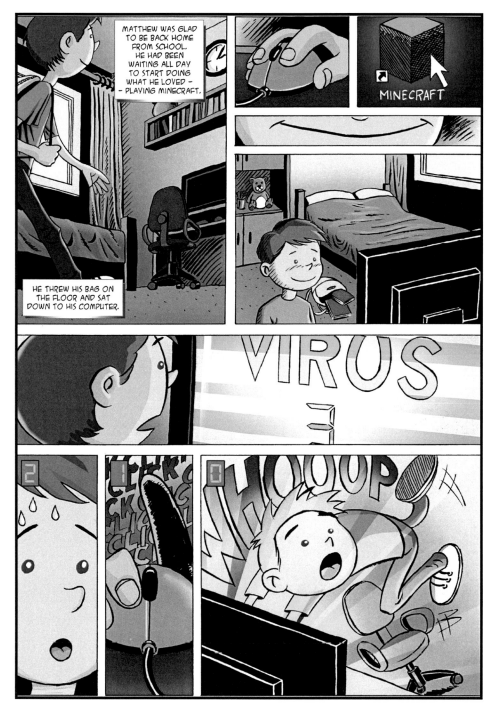

OH NO! THE VIRUS HAS SUCKED MATTHEW INTO A STRANGE PORTAL!

HE FEELS HIS BODY CHANGING...

...AND EVERYTHING AROUND HIM IS CHANGING...

WHAT JUST HAPPENED?!

AFTER TRAVELLING THROUGH A STRANGE PORTAL, MATTHEW FINDS HIMSELF IN A PLACE THAT SEEMS RATHER FARMILIAR TO HIM.

HE LOOKS AT HIS OTHER HAND, STILL TRYING TO COMPREHEND WHAT HAS JUST HAPPENED. ALL OF A SUDDEN IT STARTS TO DAWNED ON HIM...

MATTHEW DOESN'T UNDERSTAND WHAT IS GOING ON. HE STARES AT HIS RIGHT HAND WITH CONFUSION.

Matthew finally realised. He is in Minecraft! No wonder it all seemed so farmiliar to him.

Matthew hears a weird hissing noise behind him..

Matthew tries to get away as quickly as his legs can carry him.

But it is too late...

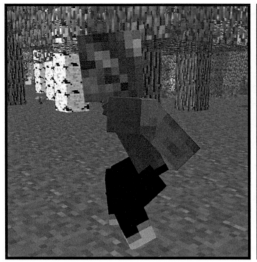

MATTHEW JUMPS JUST IN THE RIGHT MOMENT TO SAVE HIMSELF

BANG!

MATTHEW IS CATAPULTED HIGH IN THE AIR BY THE SHOCKWAVE OF THE EXPLOSION

FOR A SHORT WHILE EVERYTHING GOES DARK FOR MATHHEW

I GUESS I SHOULD EXPLORE THIS WORLD NOW...

MATTHEW DECIDES WHAT HE WILL DO NEXT

WITH THOSE WORDS SAID, MATTHEW SETS OFF ON A JOURNEY OF EXPLORATION

HE WALKED THROUGH HOT DESERTS...

...TRAVELLED THROUGH VAST SNOW BIOMES...

...AND LARGE, HUMID JUNGLES

MATTHEW CLIMBED THE HIGHEST MOUNTAINS

AFTER CLIMBING A MOUNTAIN, MATTHEW SPOTS SOME BUILDINGS IN THE DISTANCE

COULD THAT BE A CITY?!

MATTHEW SEEMS TO HAVE STUMBLED UPON A CITY

I GUESS I SHOULD GO CHECK IT OUT...

WITH EXCITEMENT MATTHEW RUSHES DOWN TO DISCOVER THIS NEW CITY

Welcome to MINETOPIA!

AS MATTHEW NEARS THE CITY, HE SEES A WELCOME SIGN.

AS MATTHEW APPROACHES THE CITY HE SEES A PERSON. IT SEEMS AS IF HE HAS BEEN WAITING FOR MATTHEW'S ARRIVAL.

GREETINGS, YOUNG MATTHEW!

HELLO...
WHAT DO YOU MEAN BY ¨EXPECTING ME¨?

After saying what he has to say, Arthur points to a statue in the distance

Matthew looked into the distance and saw a large statue of... HIMSELF

PART 2
The Great Quest

"STRANGE NOISES COMING FROM THE WOODS."

"BUT LATER ONE OF OUR VILLAGERS TOOK A WALK IN THE WOODS..."

"AND STUMBLED ACROSS A MYSTERIOUS PORTAL!"

HE DIDN'T DARE TO ENTER THE PORTAL BUT HE STOOD CLOSE ENOUGH TO OVERHEAR A CONVERSATION.

"HE HEARD **THEM** SPEAK ABOUT THEIR PLANS TO ATTACK THE VILLAGE AND TAKE OUR LAND."

WHO ARE "THEY"?

HEROBRINE AND HIS MINIONS!

"HE IS RAISING AN ARMY AND GROWING STRONGER EVERY DAY!"

YOU MUST STOP HIM MATTHEW! YOU'RE OUR ONLY HOPE!

OF COURSE I'LL HELP YOU ARTHUR! I CAN'T LET HIM DO THAT.

MATTHEW WALKS INTO HIS ROOM.

HE LOOKS AT HIS NEW BED AND A THOUGHT CROSSES HIS MIND...

MATTHEW CLOSES HIS EYES FOR 3 SECONDS... AND WHEN HE OPENS THEM IT'S MORNING.

I HOPE THERE IS SOMETHING TO EAT AROUND HERE.

MATTHEW APROACHES THE FURNACE.

AND WHEN HE LOOKS INSIDE HE FINDS A COOKED PORKCHOP.

OH, NICE!

MMM... THAT WAS DELICIOUS.

OH, I BETTER GET GOING! I NEED TO FIND THE BLACKSMITH.

MATTHEW RUNS LOOKING FOR THE BLACKSMITH. HE IS GOING TO NEED SOME ARMOR IN ORDER TO DEFEAT HEROBRINE.

SHOULD BE AROUND HERE SOMEWHERE. I CAN FEEL IT.

Matthew ventures deeper into the dark mine.

A SWIFT STAB WITH HIS SWORD SENDS THE ZOMBIE FLYING.

MATTHEW JUMPS IN THE AIR LIKE A SUPERHERO AND KICKS THE OTHER ZOMBIE IN HIS FACE!

THE ZOMBIES DIDN'T STAND A CHANGE AGAINST MATTHEW AND HIS AMAZING SKILLS.

MATTHEW EXPLORES THE CAVES EVEN FURTHER.

UNCOVERS SECRET TUNNELS.

MATTHEW FEELS THAT HE IS GETTING REALLY CLOSE.

AND THEN FINALLY...

HE GAZES UPON HEEPS OF DIAMONDS.

MATTHEW BURSTS WITH EXCITEMENT AS HE QUICKLY MINES THE DIAMOND ORE.

DIAMONDS!

MATTHEW'S QUEST FOR DIAMONDS HAS FINALLY COME TO AN END.

AFTER OBTAINING ENOUGH DIAMONDS MATTHEW RETURNS TO MR. WILSON'S WORKSHOP.

MR. WILSON!

KNOCK

KNOCK

MATTHEW IS ANXIOUS TO START CRAFTING AND MR. WILSON CAN SEE THAT. SO HE CONTINUES TO GUIDE MATTHEW THROUGH THE PROCESS.

WITH MR. WILSON'S GUIDANCE MATTHEW FORGED THE BEST ARMOR IN THE LAND AND A SWORD THAT THE GREAT NOTCH HIMSELF WOULD BE PROUD TO USE.

MATTHEW IS ALL GEARED UP LIKE A WARRIOR. HE IS ALMOST READY TO FACE HEROBRINE.

ALL HE NEEDS NOW IS AN ARMY OF HIS OWN.

THEN MATTHEW GOT AN IDEA!

MATTHEW HEADS TOWARDS MITCH'S BUTCHER SHOP. HE HAS A PLAN TO RAISE AN ARMY AND IT REQUIRES A HANDFUL OF BONES.

HE WALKED BY A PIGSTY SO MATTHEW KNEW HE WAS CLOSE.

AS A MATTER OF FACT I DO HAVE SOME LEFT OVER PIG BONES FROM YESTERDAY.

HERE YOU GO! I HOPE THIS WILL BE ENOUGH.

THIS SHOULD BE ENOUGH. THANKS!

MAY I ASK WHY DO YOU NEED ALL THESE USELESS BONES?

THE'RE NOT USELESS. THESE BONES ARE GOING TO HELP ME STOP HEROBRINE.

MATTHEW LEAVES THE SHOP WITH SOME BONES IN HIS INVENTORY AND HEADS TO THE WOODS.

HE VENTURES INTO THE WOODS TO FIND WOLVES.

HERE BOY? WHO'S A GOOD BOY?

DOESN'T TAKE TOO LONG UNTIL HE RUNS INTO A PACK OF WOLVES.

MATTHEW QUICKLY MANAGES TO TAME THE WILD BEASTS.

NOW MATTHEW HAS AN ARMY OF HIS OWN.

WHILE MATTHEW IS GATHERING HIS NEW COMPANIONS HEROBRINE IS MOVING IN FOR AN ATTACK!

HEROBRINE IS BRINGING HIS ARMY THROUGH THE PORTAL AND PREPARING FOR BATTLE! HE SEES MATTHEW WAITING FOR HIM. HEROBRINE FINDS THIS AMUSING.

AN EPIC BATTLE IS ABOUT TO BEGIN. THE FAITH OF MINETOPIA IS IN MATTHEW'S HANDS. NOTCH BE WITH HIM.

YOU ARE A FOOL TO STAND IN MY WAY! I'M GIVING YOU ONE LAST CHANCE TO SURRENDER.

I WILL NEVER SURRENDER!

VERY WELL... PREPARE TO DIE!

PART 3
The Epic Battle

MATTHEW AND HEROBRINE CLASH SWORDS TOGETHER AS THEY TRY TO STRIKE EACH OTHER!

I WILL DESTROY YOU! YOU AND YOUR PRECIOUS DOGS!

I WOULD LOVE TO SEE YOU TRY!

HEROBRINE MOVES IN FOR AN ATTACK BUT ONE OF MATTHEW'S COMPANIONS FLIES THROUGH THE AIR AND CLAMPS DOWN ON HIS ARM!

AAAAH! LET GO OF ME, YOU MUTT!!!

GOOD BOY!

WHILE HEROBRINE IS OCCUPIED WITH THE WOLVES A COUPLE OF ZOMBIE PIGMEN ATTACK MATTHEW FROM THE REAR.

MATTHEW QUICKLY REACTS AND STABS ONE OF THE ZOMBIE PIGMEN!

THE OTHER ONE GRABS MATTHEW AND TRIES TO BITE HIM!

BUT MATTHEW IS TOO FAST FOR THAT. HE SWIFTLY ESCAPES AND CHOPS OFF THE ZOMBIE PIGMAN'S ARM!

AFTER FINISHING HIM OFF MATTHEW SCANS THE AREA TO FIND WHERE HEROBRINE HAS GONE.

SUDDENLY MATTHEW RECEIVES A STRONG KICK FROM BEHIND!

HEROBRINE APROACHES MATTHEW.

MATTHEW LIES ON THE GROUND WHILE HEROBRINE SWINGS BACK HIS SWORD.

???

MATTHEW DODGES THE ATTACK!

UGH!

HE KICKS HEROBRINE IN THE STOMACH AND QUICKLY GETS BACK ON HIS FEET.

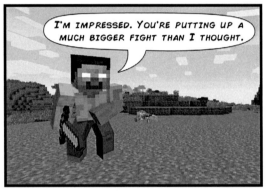

I'M IMPRESSED. YOU'RE PUTTING UP A MUCH BIGGER FIGHT THAN I THOUGHT.

THERE'S MORE WHERE THAT CAME FROM!

UNFORTUNATELY FOR YOU I LIKE A GOOD CHALLENGE.

MATTHEW AND HEROBRINE CONTINUE TO DUEL HEAD TO HEAD. THEY HAVE NOTHING ON THEIR MINDS BUT THE NEED TO DESTROY EACH OTHER.

MEANWHILE THE WOLVES ARE STARTING TO OVERPOWER THE PIGMEN. HEROBRINE'S FORCES ARE RETREATING.

WHILE MATTHEW IS STRUGGLING HIS COMPANIONS STRIKE HEROBRINE DOWN TO THE GROUND!

AS HE WATCHES HEROBRINE BEING BIT AND THROWN AROUND BY THE WOLVES MATTHEW STARTS FEELING A SENSE OF VICTORY.

FINALLY ALL THE YEARS OF PLAYING MINECRAFT ARE STARTING TO PAY OFF.

THAT'S IT! I HAVE BEEN PLAYING AROUND WITH YOU CLOWNS LONG ENOUGH!

HEROBRINE BURSTS WITH ANGER AND USES HIS TELEKINETIC POWERS TO SEND THE WOLVES FLYING!

GASP

HEROBRINE LIFTS UP A MASSIVE BLOCK OF COBBLESTONE AND THROWS IT AT MATTHEW!

UGH!

MATTHEW GETS NOCKED BACK AND HITS THE GROUND!

MATTHEW IS WEAKENED AND UNABLE TO GET UP. HIS GAMEPLAY FLASHES BEFORE HIS EYES.

HEROBRINE APPROACHES MATTHEW WITH A SMIRK ON HIS FACE.

HEROBRINE APPROACHES MATTHEW WITH A SMIRK ON HIS FACE. NOTCH KNOWS WHAT HE'LL DO TO HIM.

FOOLISH MATTHEW! YOU SHOULD HAVE LISTENED TO ME. NOW YOU'RE LAYING ON THE GROUND HELPLESS.

YOU KNOW I COULD DESTROY YOU HERE AND NOW. HOWEVER I'M NOT GOING TO DO THAT. YOU ARE WORTH MORE ALIVE THAN DEAD.

YOU'LL HAVE THE CHANCE TO SEE YOUR PRECIOUS MINETOPIA BURN!

YOU SHALL MAKE A FINE PRISONER.

HEROBRINE TAKES MATTHEW WITH HIM BACK TO THE NETHER.

AND THEN I SAID, "WHY DON'T YOU CHECK IF THE LAVA IS WARM!?"

BACK AT THE NETHER...

HEROBRINE COMES THROUGH THE PORTAL WITH HIS NEW PRISONER.

HEROBRINE AND HIS MINIONS RETURN TO THEIR LAIR. MATTHEW IS BARELY CONSCIOUS AND CAN ONLY HEAR RANDOM MUMBLING AS THEY ENTER THE FORTRESS.

IN YOU GO!

UGH!

THE ZOMBIE PIGMAN THROWS MATTHEW IN HIS CELL.

IN YOU GO!

UGH!

THE ZOMBIE PIGMAN THROWS MATTHEW IN HIS CELL.

YOU HAVE MADE THIS MORE COMPLICATED THAN IT SHOULD BE.

BOSS IS NOT HAPPY ABOUT THIS.

GOOD NIGHT CHOSEN ONE! HE HE HE.

MEANWHILE HEROBRINE IS RESTING IN HIS QUARTERS.

THINKING ABOUT HOW MATTHEW HAS BEEN A SETBACK IN HIS PLAN.

SOME TIME PASSES AND MATTHEW WAKES UP. HE FINDS HIMSELF IN A DIRTY PRISON CELL.

WHA... WHERE AM I?

YOU'RE IN HEROBRINE'S DUNGEON.

WHAT?

YEAH, YOU'VE BEEN CAPTURED AND LOCKED UP JUST LIKE ME. ALL BECAUSE YOU WERE TRYING TO DO THE RIGHT THING AND SAVE A CITY.

HOW DO YOU KNOW THAT?

I'VE HEARD SOME RUMOURS AROUND HERE FROM THE ZOMBIE PIGS. HOW YOU'RE SUPPOSED TO BE THE CHOSEN ONE. I WAS THE CHOSEN ONE ONCE, YOU KNOW.

WHAT DO YOU MEAN?

IT ALL HAPPENED A FEW YEARS AGO...

"I WAS SCOUTING THE AREA FOR RESOURCES AND STUMBLED ACROSS A SMALL VILLAGE CALLED MINEVILLE."

"THE VILLAGE ELDER TOLD ME ABOUT HOW THEY WERE HEARING STRANGE NOISES FROM THE WOODS AND THAT THE VILLAGE IS IN DANGER."

"AFTER HEARING ALL THAT I AGREED TO HELP THEM."

LITTLE DID I KNOW THAT I WAS ABOUT TO MAKE THE BIGGEST MISTAKE OF MY LIFE.

SO YOU'VE BEEN HERE FOR YEARS? ISN'T THERE A WAY OUT?

MANY HAVE TRIED AND FAILED.

I HAVE NOT YET PUT MYSELF IN THAT CATEGORY.

WELL THERE'S GOT TO BE A WAY TO ESCAPE!

THERE'S ALWAYS A WAY...

HEROBRINE AND THE PRISON GUARD HEAD TOWARDS MATTHEW'S CELL.

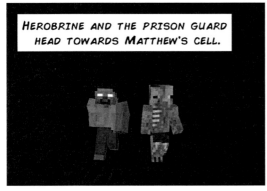

HEROBRINE ENTERS THE CELL BLOCK AND HE CAN'T BELIEVE HIS EYES.

MATTHEW AND DUNCAN HAVE ESCAPED!!!

PART 4
Prison Break

Not much time passes and one of the castle's watchmen approach Herobrine.

While Herobrine is exchanging words with the watchman, a messenger rushes in.

LITTLE DID HEROBRINE AND HIS MINIONS KNOW THAT MATTHEW AND DUNCAN ESCAPED MORE THAN 3 HOURS AGO.

MATTHEW GETS DISTRACTED AS HE HEARS FOOTSTEPS FROM THE HALLWAY.

A PRISON GUARD ENTERS AND GAZES UPON THE SLEEPING PRISONERS.

HE LEAVES SHORTLY AFTER SEEING THAT EVERYTHING IS IN ORDER.

HERE YOU GO, FRIEND.

MATTHEW PICKS UP THE PLANKS AND QUICKLY CRAFTS A CRAFTING TABLE.

AND NOW WE JUST HAVE TO DO A LITTLE MINING. HE HE.

MATTHEW WASTES NO TIME AND CRAFTS A WOODEN PICKAXE.

MATTHEW STARTS DIGGING A HOLE IN THE FLOOR.

AAH... THAT'S BEAUTIFUL.

SEE? I TOLD YOU THERE IS ALWAYS A WAY!

LET'S GO!

THAT'S A DECENT DROP RIGHT THERE.

MATTHEW AND DUNCAN DIG THROUGH THE SIDE OF THE CASTLE AND FIND THEMSELVES QUITE HIGH UP.

MATTHEW DIGS OUT A STAIRWAY IN THE SIDE OF THE CASTLE SO THEY CAN GET DOWN SAFELY.

Matthew and Duncan manage to jump away from the blast.

???

The explosion destroys the portal and blows the pigmen sky high!

Woah, that was close.

The Gast is still coming for us! We need to find cover!

Matthew and Duncan run behind a big mountain.

Ok, I think it's gone. We are safe for now.

But how are we going to get back home? The portal is ruined.

I don't know. We have to find a way to repair the portal or build a new one.

Ok, let's get a move on.

OUR HEROES TRAVEL FURTHER ALONG THE FLAMING POOLS OF LAVA, SEARCHING FOR A WAY OUT.

MATTHEW, LOOK OUT! A ZOMBIE PIGMAN!

RELAX. THESE ARE NOT HEROBRINE'S MINIONS. THEY'RE NEUTRAL MOBS.

THEY WON'T ATTACK UNLESS WE DO.

YOU SURE KNOW A LOT ABOUT THIS PLACE, MATTHEW.

LOOK OVER THERE!

A CAVE. LET'S GO CHECK IT OUT.

MATTHEW AND DUNCAN HEAD INTO THE CAVE.

THEY COULD NOT HAVE GONE FAR. WE MUST TRACK THEM DOWN!

MEANWHILE HEROBRINE IS ON THEIR TRAIL.

WE WILL, MY LORD.

IT LOOKS LIKE SOMEONE'S BEEN HERE RECENTLY.

MATTHEW AND DUNCAN FIND THEMSELVES IN A MYSTERIOUS TUNNEL.

LOOK, THERE'S A ROOM JUST UP AHEAD.

WOW. THIS MUST BE A PART TIME BASE.

I WONDER WHO MADE IT.

WELL, I DON'T KNOW ABOUT THAT, BUT I'M SURE HE WON'T MIND IF WE BORROW SOME OF HIS STUFF.

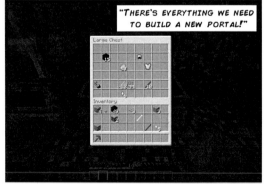

"THERE'S EVERYTHING WE NEED TO BUILD A NEW PORTAL!"

MATTHEW AND DUNCAN START PLACING BLOCKS AS FAST AS THEY CAN.

ONE OF HEROBRINE'S MINIONS WALK INTO THE ROOM.

DUNCAN INTERRUPTS THE PIGMAN BY PUNCHING HIM IN THE FACE!

TO BE CONTINUED...

Made in the USA
San Bernardino, CA
24 July 2015